MLU Play

Coloring Book

SKYD PRESS

Seattle, Washington

MLU Play is a United States 501c3 non-profit organization committed to reducing barriers to play ultimate.

For enthusiastic Elliott, literate Lydia and tolerant Tessa

MLU Play Coloring Book
Color with your favorite Major League Ultimate teams
ISBN 978-0-9963107-0-3

©2015 Confluence for Major Ultimate LLC
Conceived, assembled and edited by Daniel M. Vogel
Published by Skyd Press, the Printed Voice of Ultimate.
  http://**skyd.press**
  http://**skydmagazine.com**

Printed in the United States of America
First Edition

My name is

_____

_____.

I am _____ years old.

My favorite MLU team is the

_____;

Someday, I want to be a

_____

for the team!

Design Your Own!

Why should the league have all the fun designing discs and jerseys?

In this book are blank discs and jerseys. Send your best work to

DesignYourOwn@MLUltimate.com

or post it on Twitter or Instagram with

#MLUPlay

Major League Ultimate and MLU Play

may actually make limited editions of

the best discs and jersey submissions!

Download additional blanks and other pages at

http://coloring.mluplay.com

Design Your Own Disc!

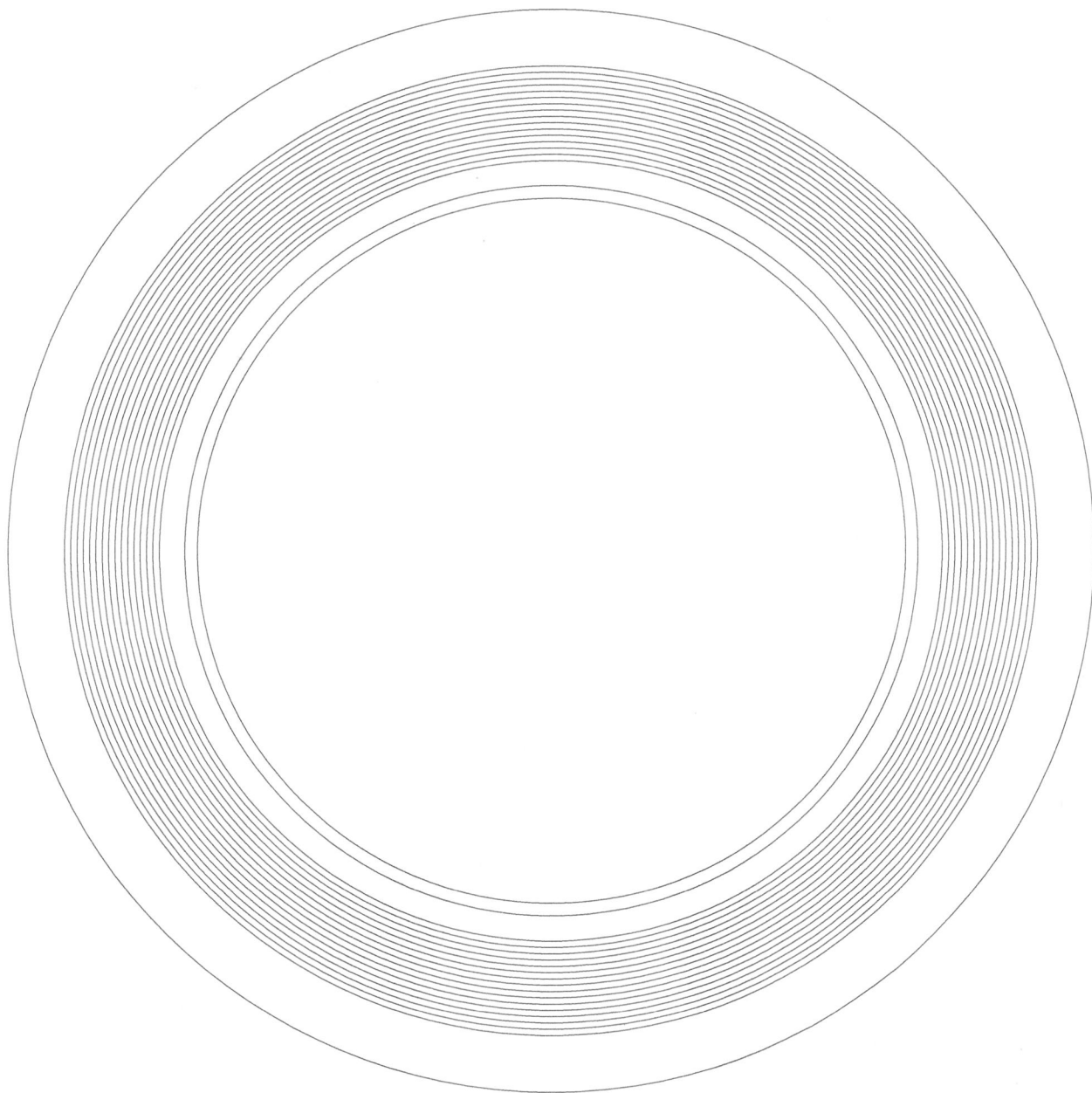

Send your designs to designyourown@mlultimate.com

Design Your Own Jersey!

Send your designs to designyourown@mlultimate.com

The Pull

The Cutter

The Handler

The Mark

Defense!

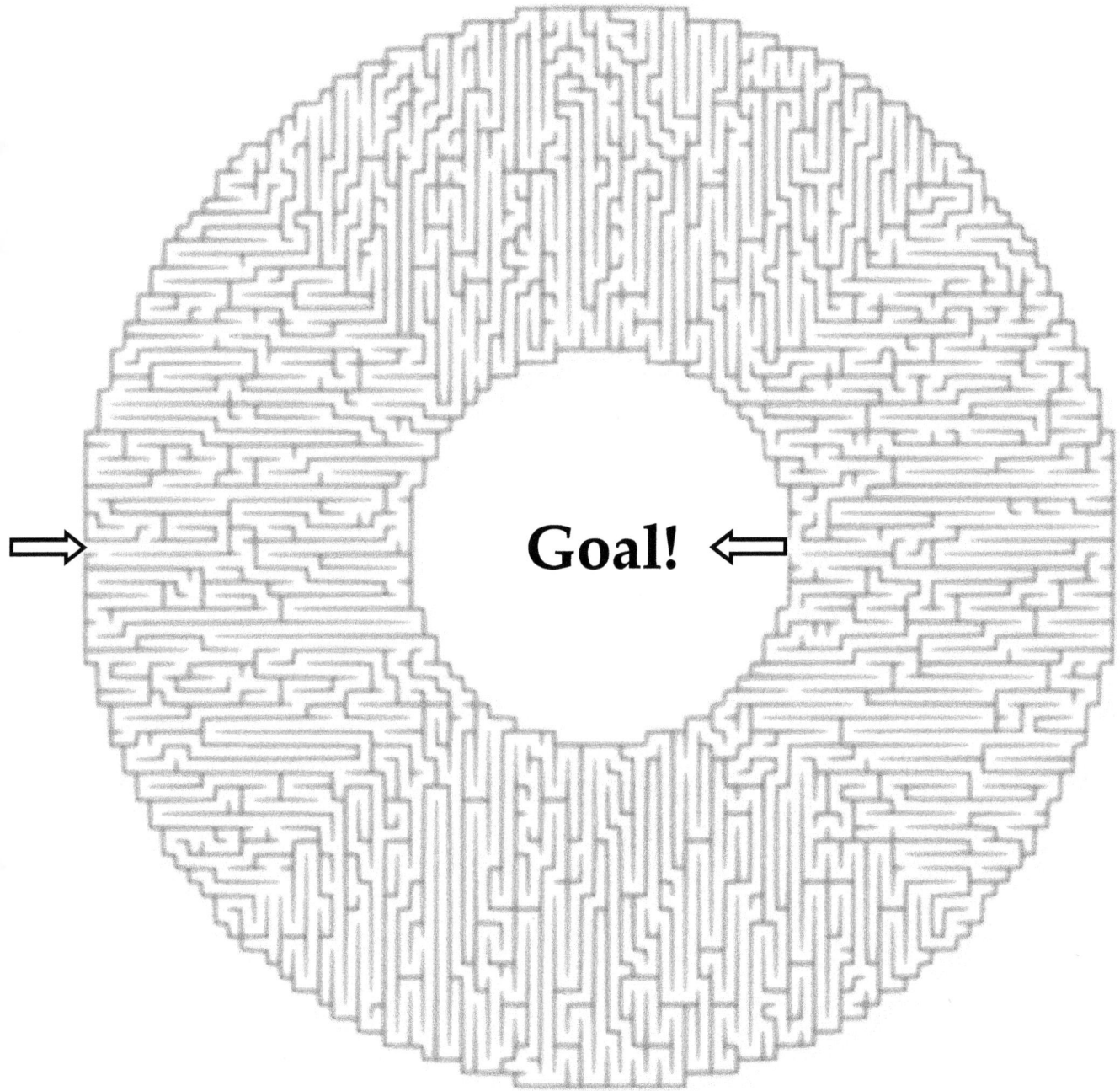

Goal!

Western Conference Teams

☆ **Vancouver**
Nighthawks

☆ **Seattle**
Rainmakers

☆ **Portland**
Stags

☆ **San Francisco**
Dogfish

```
B  U  F  A  E  V  H  G  T  W  X  S
F  T  I  V  X  S  G  A  T  S  A  L
V  A  N  C  O  U  V  E  R  N  N  E
D  S  B  F  T  T  D  E  F  I  T  V
N  H  W  F  F  O  K  R  G  Q  P  B
N  O  D  G  G  A  A  H  Z  I  C  G
D  I  T  F  M  N  T  G  K  D  S  B
C  Q  I  N  C  H  Z  L  W  Y  M  K
N  S  I  I  A  C  Q  W  T  X  V  R
H  A  S  W  E  X  B  M  B  J  W  Z
R  C  K  P  O  R  T  L  A  N  D  Y
O  S  P  N  Z  E  L  T  T  A  E  S
```

- Vancouver
- Seattle
- Portland
- ~~San Francisco~~
- Nighthawks
- Rainmakers
- Stags
- Dogfish

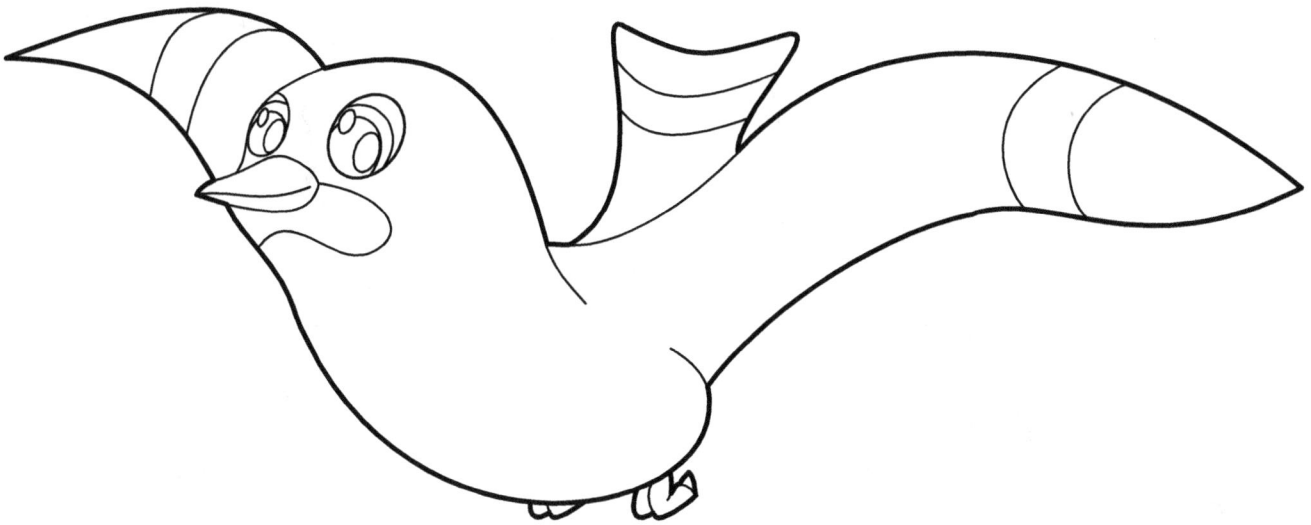

Mo Hawkins

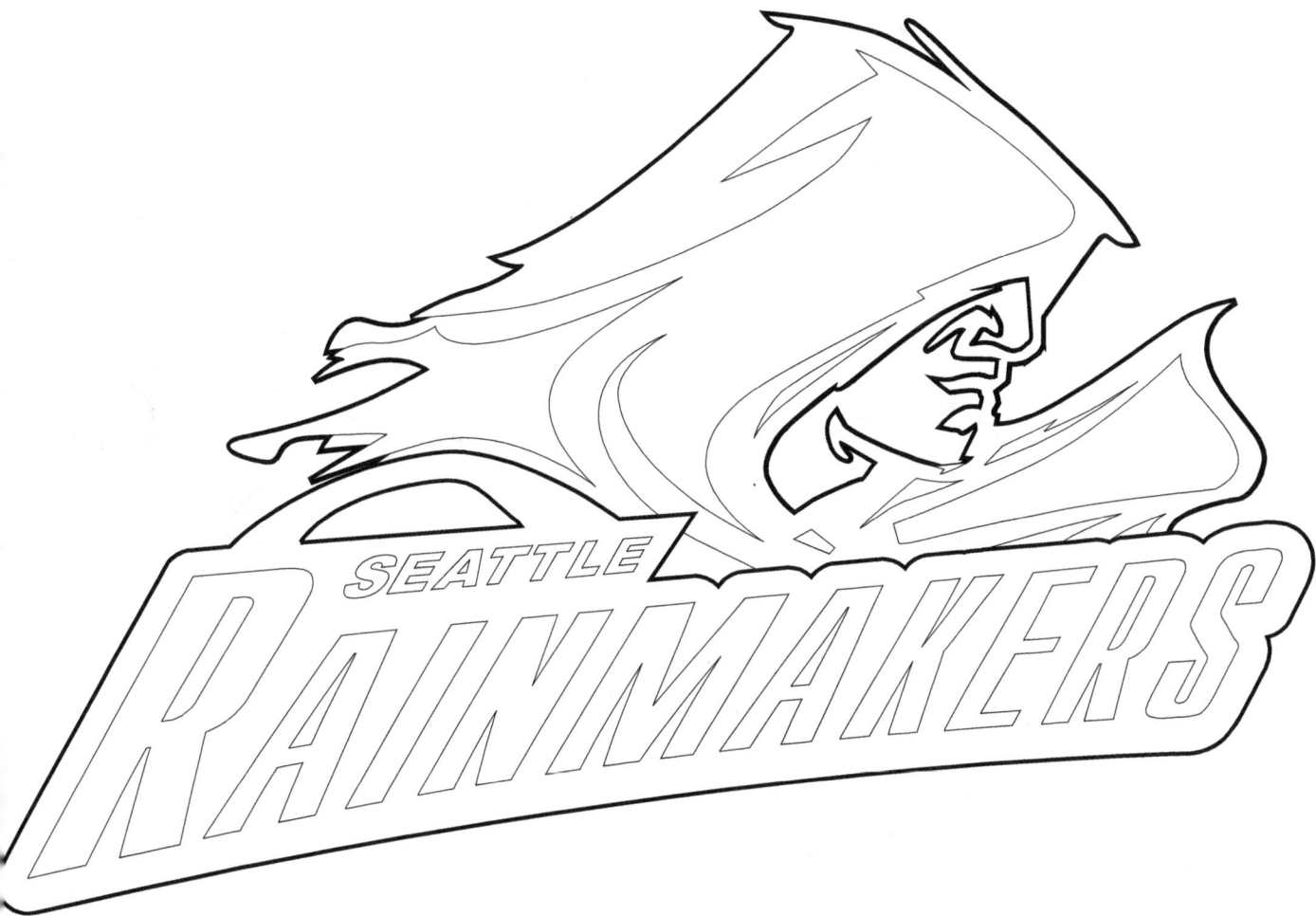

Stags

PORTLAND

Dougie the Dogfish

Eastern Conference Teams

Boston
Whitecaps

New York
Rumble

Philadelphia
Spinners

Washington DC
Current

```
R  O  X  K  H  P  W  Q  U  G  F  H
Y  A  F  S  Q  H  A  K  M  J  I  M
V  J  A  P  C  I  S  R  A  G  U  T
J  P  K  A  U  L  H  O  B  R  X  N
X  Y  P  C  N  A  I  Y  O  Q  S  E
K  T  F  E  O  D  N  W  S  L  P  R
X  A  E  T  J  E  G  E  T  A  I  R
L  Y  L  I  K  L  T  N  O  I  N  U
N  D  B  H  O  P  O  W  N  Q  N  C
V  E  M  W  R  H  N  Q  U  W  E  A
Y  V  U  H  Z  I  D  P  S  X  R  V
I  Z  R  F  Q  A  C  B  A  G  S  D
```

- Boston
- New York
- Philadelphia
- Washington DC
- Whitecaps
- Rumble
- Spinners
- Current

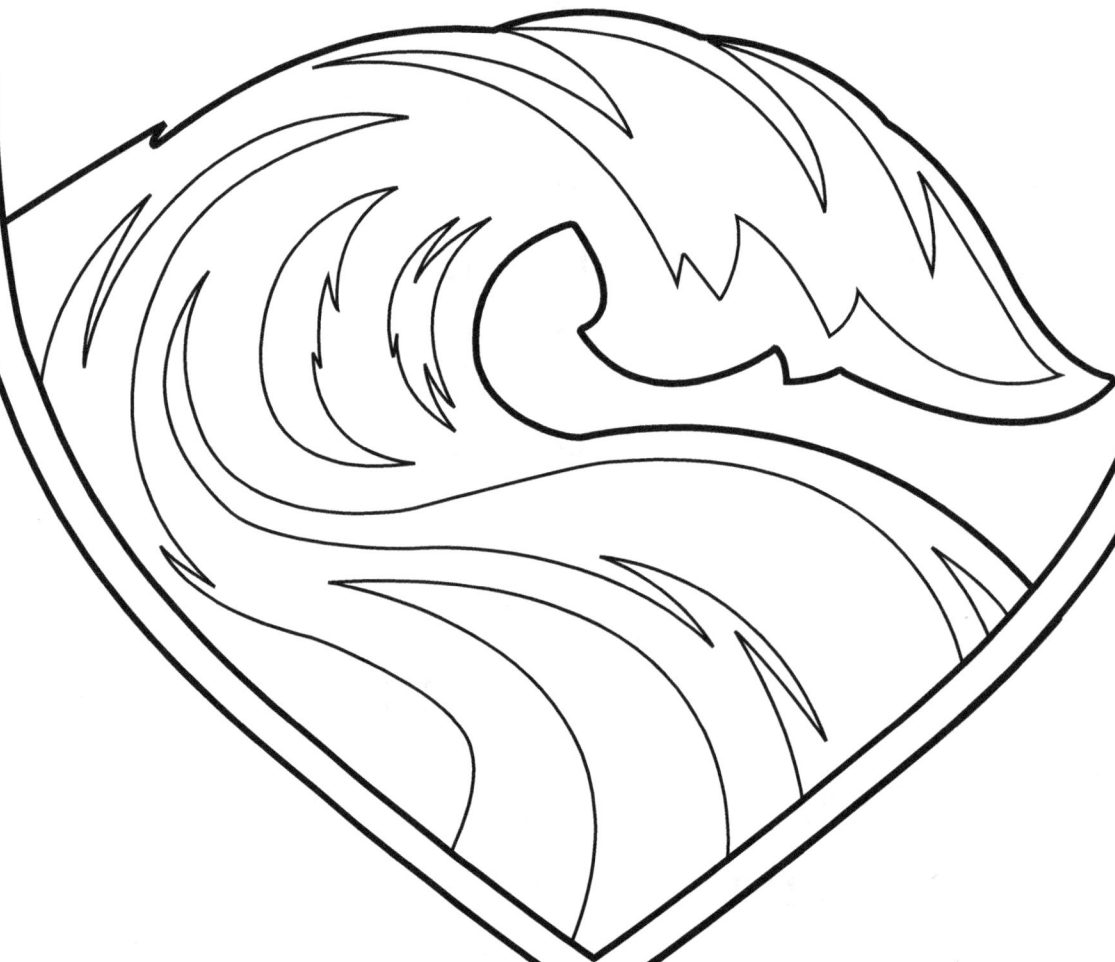

WHITECAPS
BOSTON

WHITECAPS BOSTON

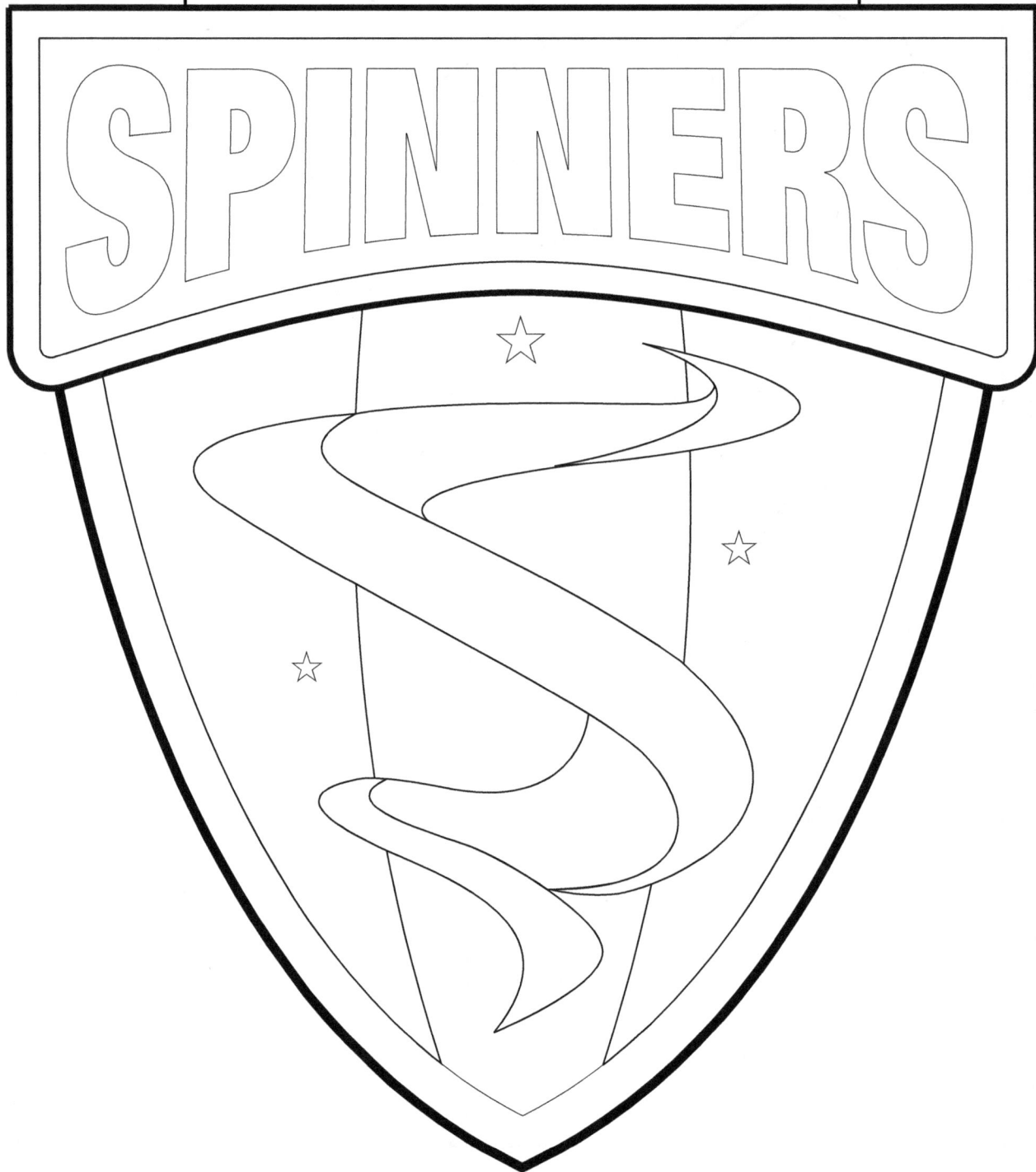
PHILADELPHIA
SPINNERS

Dizzy

DC Dojo Cowbell

ML

MAJOR LEAGUE ULTIMATE

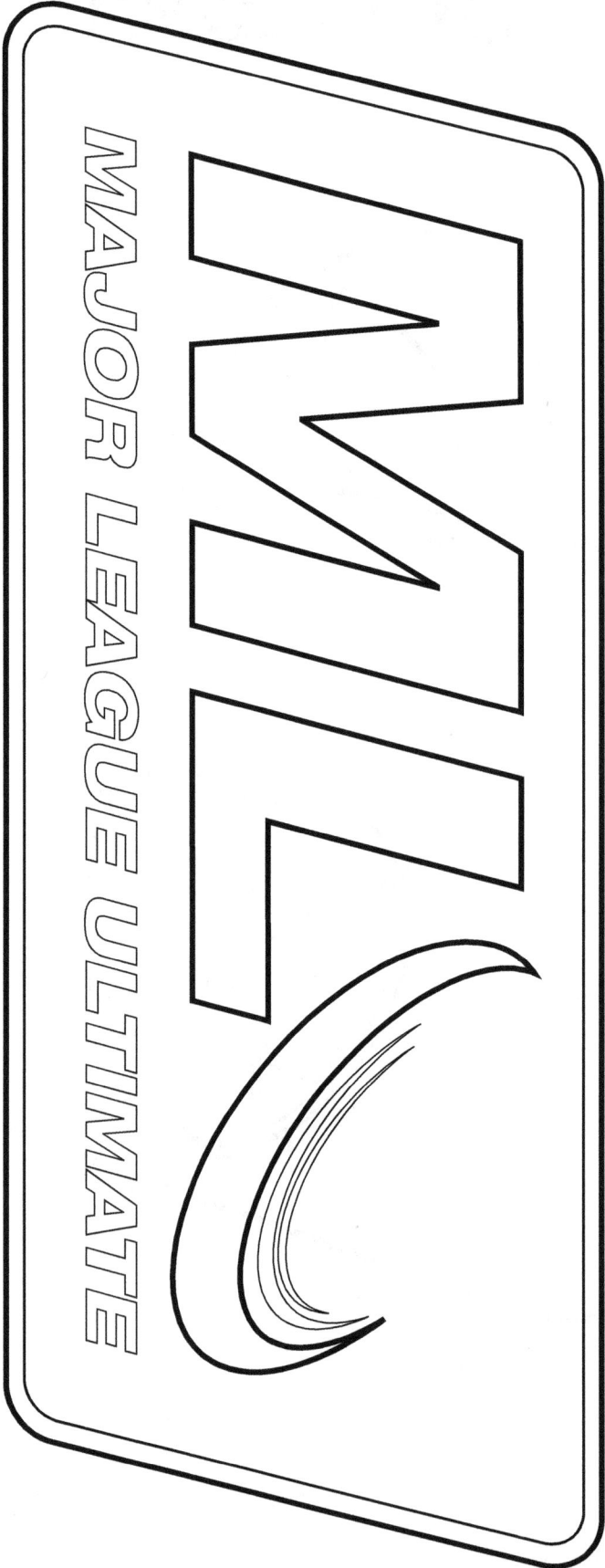

The Championship Trophy

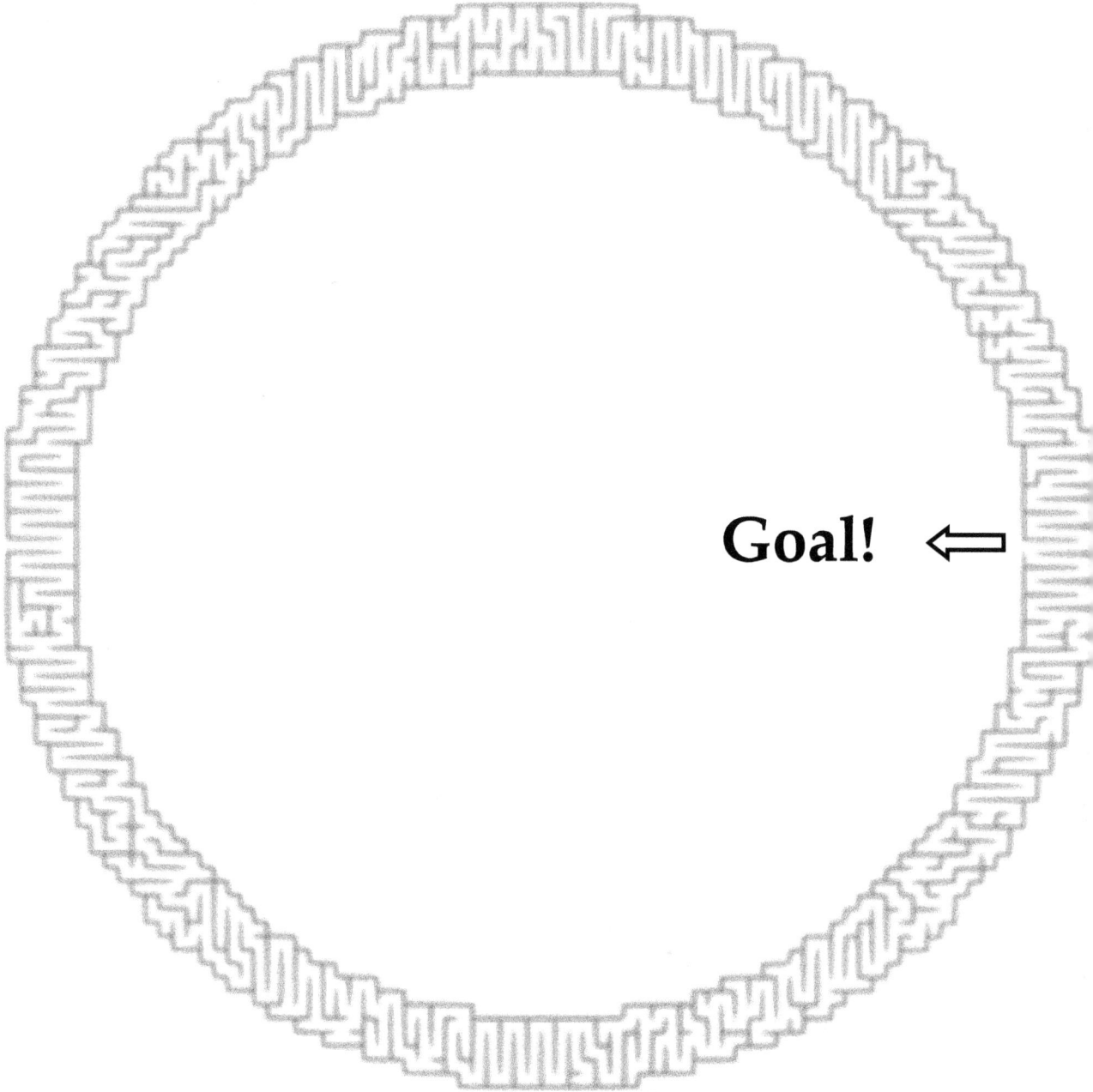

Goal!

Design Your Own Disc!

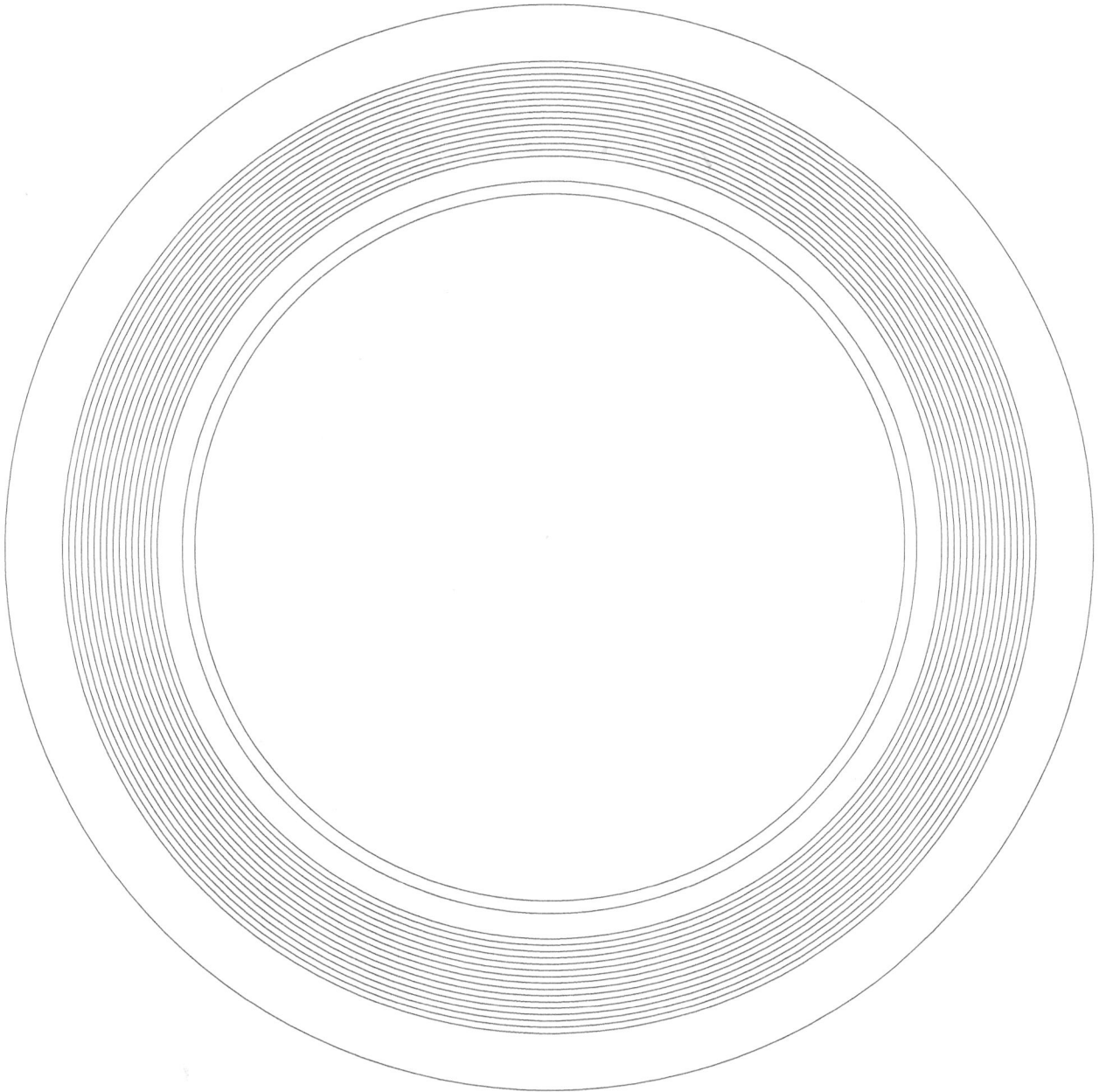

Send your designs to designyourown@mlultimate.com

Design Your Own Jersey!

Send your designs to designyourown@mlultimate.com

What to expect at the game

Double team

Someone is open

Listen to the Refs!

Timeout!

After the game, players shake

and greet fans

Design Your Own Disc!

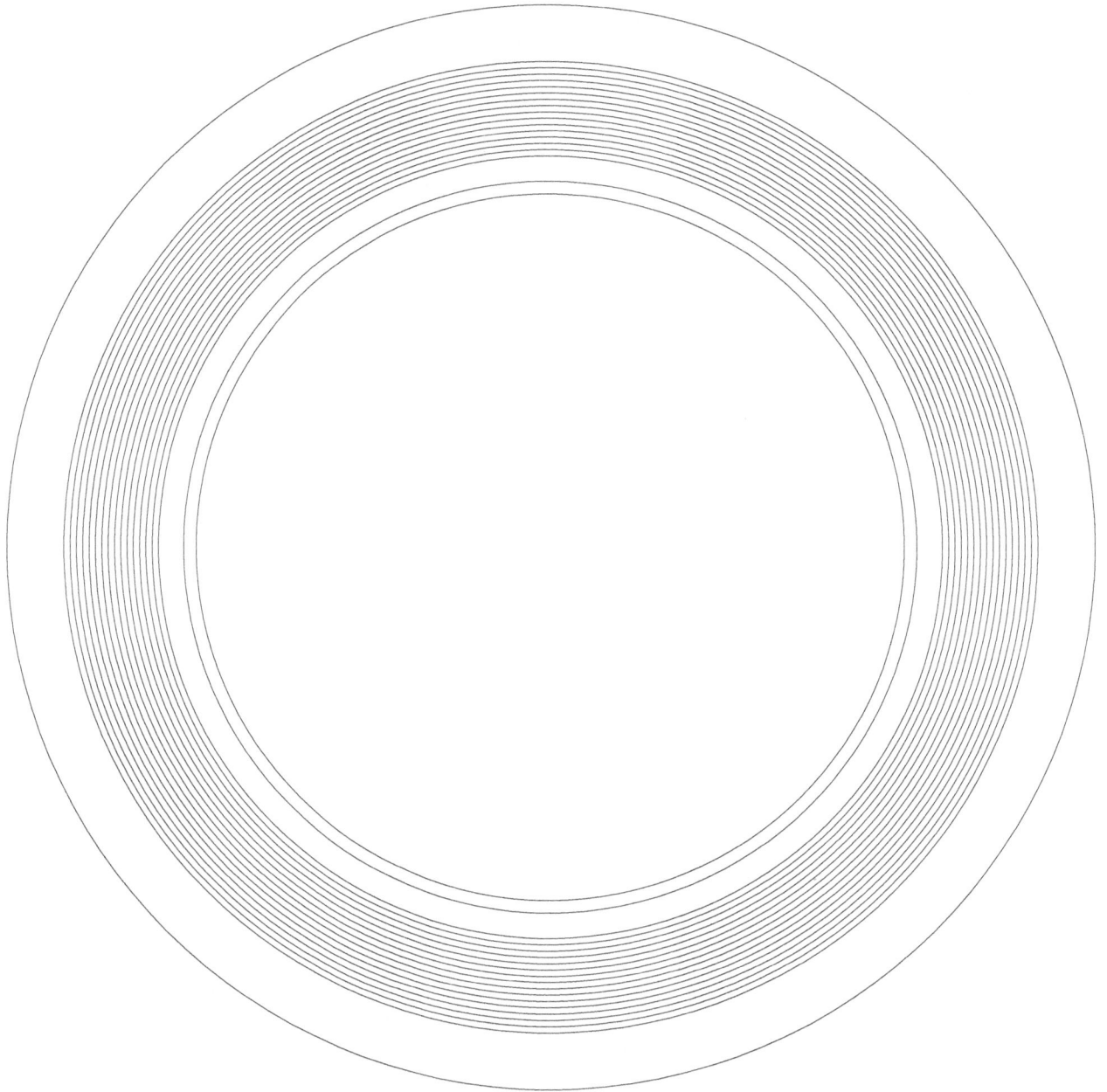

Send your designs to designyourown@mlultimate.com

Design Your Own Jersey!

Send your designs to designyourown@mlultimate.com

This coloring book was a global effort. Thank you for your purchase.

Design Credits:

    Dan Vogel

    Nic Darling of Philadelphia, PA

    Matthew 'Skip' Sewell of Seattle, WA

    Cover by Adam Restad of Billings, MT

    Layout by Megha at SWSIndia of Punjab, India

Art Credits:

    Dan Vogel

    Dave Terry of Victorville, CA USA, http://www.dave-terry.com

    Dusty Mellings of Medicine Hat, AB Canada

    Crazy Animation of Kolkata, India

    Hugo Lazo F. of Lima, Peru

    James Ryan Belgira of Quezon City, Philippines

    Dao Kim Phuc of Ho Chi Minh City, Vietnam

Puzzles:

    Dan Vogel

    Mazes generated with Puzzlemaker from Discovery Education

        http://www.discoveryeducation.com/puzzlemaker

To the hardworking, dedicated oneironauts who make Major League Ultimate.

Learn more about Major League Ultimate
On the web at **mlultimate.com**
Twitter **@MLUltimate**
Facebook.com/**MLUltimate**